Jamestown

Hands-on Projects About One of America's First Communities

Jennifer Quasha

The Rosen Publishing Group's
PowerKids Press™

Some of the projects in this book were designed for a child to do together with an adult.

For Chris, who lives in her own "Jamestown."

Published in 2001 by The Rosen Publishing Group, Inc.
29 East 21st Street, New York, NY 10010

First Edition

Book Design: Felicity Erwin

Layout: Michael de Guzman

Photo Credits: p. 4 © North Wind Picture Archives; pp. 6 – 21 by Pablo Maldonado.

Quasha, Jennifer.
    Jamestown : hands-on projects about one of America's first communities / Jennifer Quasha.— 1st ed.
      p. cm.— (Great social studies projects)
    Includes index.
    Summary: An introduction to the first English settlement at Jamestown, Virginia, with step-by-step instructions for a variety of related projects including a topographical map of the settlement, a model Jamestown house, and wooden spoon puppets.
    ISBN 0-8239-5701-2 (alk. paper)
    1. Jamestown (Va.)—History—17th century—Study and teaching—Activity programs—Juvenile literature. 2. Jamestown (Va.)—Social life and customs—17th century—Study and teaching—Activity programs—Juvenile literature. 3. Virginia—History—Colonial period, ca. 1600–1775—Study and teaching—Activity programs—Juvenile literature. [1. Jamestown (Va.)—History—17th century. 2. Jamestown (Va.)—Social life and customs—17th century. 3. Virginia—History—Colonial period, ca. 1600–1775.] I. Title.

F234.J3 Q37 2000
975.5'425101—dc21   00-024315

Manufactured in the United States of America

Contents

Jamestown

Jamestown was America's first permanent English **settlement**. The people who traveled from England to early America were very brave. They did not know what they would find when they arrived. They dreamed of finding **fertile** land to grow crops. They even hoped to find gold. What they found instead was a hard life. Many people died because there was not enough food to eat, the weather was very cold, and there were attacks by Native Americans. In fact, more than half of the **settlers** died within four months of arriving in Jamestown. At one point the settlers packed up their ships to sail home. At the last minute they decided to stay. It took many years for Jamestown to become a successful colony.

Life was hard in the early days of Jamestown, the first permanent English settlement.

5

Three Ships Diorama

On December 20, 1606, three ships set sail from England for America. Their names were *Susan Constant*, *Godspeed*, and *Discovery*. The three ships carried 144 men and boys. The trip had been organized by the Virginia Company. The king of England, James I, had given the Virginia Company **permission** to start an English colony in America. Four months after the ships left England, they arrived on American soil.

Here's how to make a **diorama** of the three ships:

tools and materials

- one shoe box, without lid
- four sheets of blue construction paper
- clear tape
- scissors
- one sheet of brown construction paper
- one sheet of white construction paper
- three Popsicle sticks

1 Cover the upside down shoe box with blue construction paper by taping it on with clear tape.

 2 Using scissors, poke three slits into the bottom of the covered shoe box.

 3 Using the brown construction paper, cut out the three ships. Using the white construction paper, cut out the sails. Tape the ships and sails onto the top half of the Popsicle sticks.

 4 Slip the bottom half of the Popsicle sticks into the slits in the shoe box.

Native American Tomahawk

On May 14, 1607, the three ships of English settlers arrived on the shores of America. They found that the land was **inhabited** by Native Americans from the Powhatan Confederacy. The Powhatan Confederacy was a group of more than 30 **tribes** all under the leadership of a Native American chief named Powhatan. Some of the Native Americans were friendly. Others fought with the English settlers. Native Americans used tomahawks in battles. Here's how to make your own tomahawk:

tools and materials

- scissors
- two 6" x 6" (15 x 15 cm) pieces of cardboard
- woodworking glue
- one 36" x 1" x ⁵⁄₁₆" (91 x 2.5 x .8 cm) piece of balsa wood
- aluminum foil

1 Cut out the shape of a tomahawk blade from a piece of cardboard. Trace the shape onto the second piece of cardboard and cut out a second tomahawk blade shape.

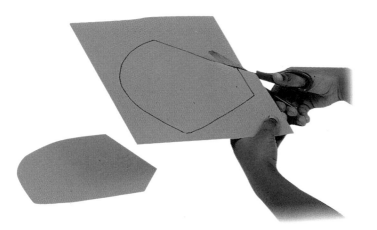

2 Glue one blade to each side of the wooden stick. Keep half an inch (1.3 cm) of the wooden handle visible above the blade. Let dry.

3 When dry, wrap aluminum foil over the blade.

Land Map of Jamestown

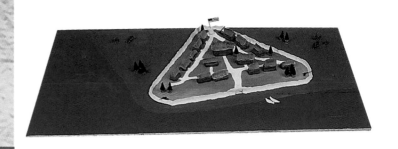

When the English settlers arrived, they built a protected settlement along the river. They built a guard wall to protect the settlement from the Native Americans. The settlers chopped down trees to create a **triangular** wall around the settlement. The walls of the fort were 420 feet (128 m) long on the river side and 300 feet (91 m) long on each of the other two sides.

Here's how to make your own land map of Jamestown:

tools and materials

- 16" x 24" (41 x 61 cm) piece of plywood
- paintbrush
- acrylic or poster paint
- molding clay
  (Clay that dries overnight and does not need to be baked works best.)
- 5 black toothpicks
- white glue or clear tape
- miniature trees, animals, etc.

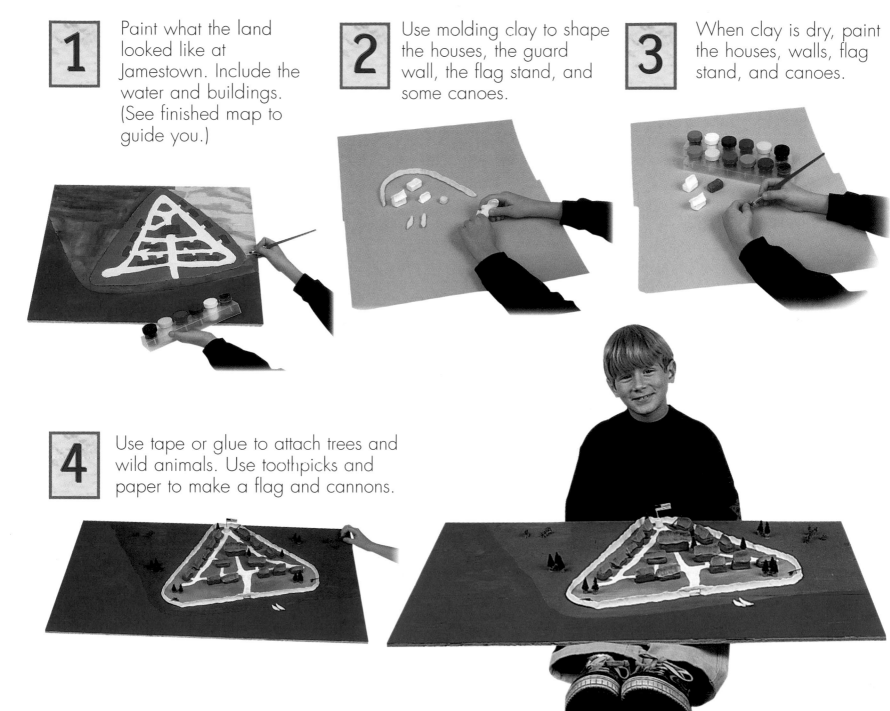

1 Paint what the land looked like at Jamestown. Include the water and buildings. (See finished map to guide you.)

2 Use molding clay to shape the houses, the guard wall, the flag stand, and some canoes.

3 When clay is dry, paint the houses, walls, flag stand, and canoes.

4 Use tape or glue to attach trees and wild animals. Use toothpicks and paper to make a flag and cannons.

Model of a Jamestown House

After the guard walls were in place, the settlers began to build their colony. During the day they chopped down trees. They also gathered grass and straw. The men used the wood from the trees to make the walls of their houses. They dried the grass and straw and used them to make **thatched** roofs. By June 15, 1607, the settlers had completed their task. They all had homes. Here's how to use Popsicle sticks and **raffia** to make your own Jamestown house:

tools and materials

- waxed paper
- white glue
- 112 Popsicle sticks
- paintbrush
- brown and white paint
- raffia
- white paper

Lay out waxed paper. On the waxed paper, glue together two rows of 18 Popsicle sticks. Then glue two rows of 15 sticks, and another two rows of 20 sticks. These six strips of sticks will make the four sides and roof of the house.

 On the end of each row, on top of the last stick, glue an extra Popsicle stick.

After the Popsicle-stick rows are dry, glue the walls of the house together using the two rows of 18 sticks and the two rows of 15 sticks. To make the roof, join the two rows of 20 sticks together in an upside-down "V" shape. Connect with glue and strip of waxed paper.

 Paint the outside of the house using the brown paint. Add windows and a door using white paint. Glue the raffia onto the roof.

Wooden Spoon Puppets

Captain John Smith was an early leader of Jamestown. English settlers often **sparred** with Native Americans. Smith tried to make peace with the Powhatan Confederacy by talking with their leader, Powhatan. The two leaders didn't always agree. Once, Powhatan held Smith prisoner and planned to kill him. Powhatan's daughter, Pocahontas, saved Smith by lying on top of him. To kill Smith, her father would have had to kill her too. She saved Smith's life! Here's how to make puppets of Smith and Pocahontas:

tools and materials

- two wooden spoons
- four Popsicle sticks
- acrylic paint
- paintbrush
- yarn for hair
- white glue
- six pieces of felt; one piece each of brown, yellow, red, orange, white, and blue.
- feathers and two sets of googly eyes
- scissors
- double-sided clear tape

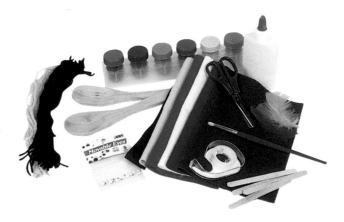

Paint both wooden spoons and all four Popsicle sticks. Use the colors shown below.

When paint is dry, glue on yarn for hair. Glue on googly eyes.

Fold brown and blue pieces of felt in half. Cut two-sided outfits out of felt to make both John's suit and Pocahontas's dress. Cut out collars, cuffs, belts, and a bag from the remaining felt colors.

4
Place double-sided clear tape on the handle of one spoon, on the two Popsicle sticks of the same color, and on John's felt outfit. Then stick the two sides of the outfit onto each side of the handle of the spoon. Add clothing details, such as collar and cuffs. Repeat these steps for Pocahontas.

Beeswax Candle and Candleholder

There was no **electricity** in the 1600s, so the people of Jamestown needed to find another way to see after dark. The settlers worked during daylight hours and went to sleep when it got dark. They needed candles for nighttime emergencies. **Beeswax** candles were made from the beeswax the settlers collected at a bee-keeping farm. **Pewter** candleholders were sometimes brought from England. Here's how to make your own beeswax candle:

tools and materials

- one 8" x 8" (20 x 20 cm) sheet of beeswax
- one candlewick
- scissors
- one 8" x 11" (20 x 28 cm) piece of cardboard
- masking tape
- aluminum foil
  (DO NOT LIGHT A CANDLE WITHOUT AN ADULT'S HELP.)

1 Roll the sheet of beeswax around the candlewick.

2 Cut a four-inch (10-cm) circle and two 4" x 1" (10 x 2.5 cm) strips from the cardboard.

3 Wrap one of the strips of cardboard around the base of the candle. Use masking tape to make a cardboard tube that fits around the candle. Tape tube to the center of cardboard circle.

4 Fold other strip of cardboard in half for handle. Tape to circle's edge. Cover base and handle with foil.

Hornbook for School

After many years, Jamestown became a **thriving** community with its own school. Jamestown children used hornbooks at school to learn the alphabet. A hornbook was shaped like a wooden paddle. Since paper was rare, the letters were often scratched into white birch bark nailed to the paddle. To protect the bark, a thin layer of horn was nailed on top. This is how the hornbook got its name. Here's how to make a hornbook:

tools and materials

- one ³⁄₁₆" x 6" x 36" (.4 x 15 x 91 cm) piece of balsa wood
- X-Acto knife
- thin black permanent marker
- one 5 ½" x 7 ½" (14 x 19 cm) sheet paper
- white glue
- paintbrush
- decoupage glaze
- scissors

1 Cut balsa wood into a 6" x 12" (15 x 30 cm) rectangle. Measure 8" (20 cm) down and 2" (5 cm) in on each of the 12" (30 cm) sides. Then cut in 2" (5 cm). From 2" (5 cm) in, cut down 4". (10 cm). This leaves a handle for the hornbook.

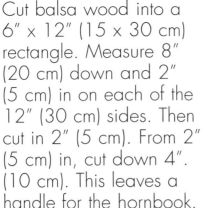

2 Using the black marker, write the alphabet and numbers one through nine, and draw a small design on the white paper.

3 Using white glue, glue paper onto the hornbook.

4 When glue is dry, paint two layers of decoupage glaze onto the paper for protection.

Quilt Square

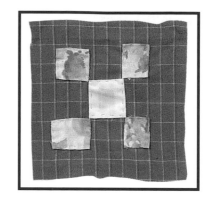

In order to keep their families warm in the cold winter, women made quilts. They used cloth that was sent over from England. They used pieces of old clothing, too. Women sewed with needles and thread that were also brought from England. Often, many women would sew together in a group, called a bee, or a sewing bee. Sometimes they would work on their own projects. Other times they would all work on the same project. Here's how to make your own quilt square:

tools and materials

- pinking shears
- at least two scraps of fabric in two different designs
- pins
- white thread
- needle
- an 8″ x 8″ (20 x 20 cm) piece of fabric

Using pinking shears, cut two-inch (5.1-cm) squares from the scraps of fabric. From one scrap, cut one square. From the second scrap, cut four squares.

 Fold over the edges of the small squares and pin them so the pinking-shear edges are covered.

Thread the needle and sew the small fabric squares onto the large fabric square in the design shown below. Remember to remove the pins you put in (in step two) before you sew all the way around each square.

How to Use Your Projects

You have made some terrific projects about the people, places, and things from the early American community of Jamestown. You can use these projects for school, fun, or decoration. Does your classroom need some decoration? Volunteer to bring in your three ships diorama. Does your little sister or brother know the exciting story of Captain John Smith and Pocahontas? You can use the wooden spoon puppets to teach them some American history. How about giving the beeswax candle as a birthday gift to your mom or dad? Maybe you can use the hornbook to practice spelling words with a classmate. Have fun with your projects. Remember, they are a great way to understand how life was different in the early days of America!

Glossary

beeswax (BEEZ-wax) Wax that is made by bees.

colony (KAH-luh-nee) An area in a new country where a large group of people live together, who are still ruled by the leaders and laws of their old country.

decoupage glaze (DAY-KOO-pahj GLAYZ) Clear polish used to make something shiny.

diorama (dy-uh-RA-muh) A small version of a natural scene created by using lifelike details and a painted background.

electricity (ih-lek-TRIH-sih-tee) A form of energy that can produce light, heat, or motion.

fertile (FUR-tul) Good for making and growing things.

inhabited (in-HA-bit-id) Lived in.

permission (pur-MIH-shun) The act of allowing someone to do something.

pewter (PYEW-ter) A dull, bluish-gray metal made out of lead.

raffia (RAH-fee-uh) Part of the raffia plant that is often used for making baskets and hats.

settlers (SEH-tuh-lerz) People who move to a new land to live.

settlement (SEH-tul-ment) A small village or group of houses.

sparred (SPARD) To have fought small fights.

thatched (THACHD) Made of twigs, grass, and bark bundled together.

thriving (THRYV-ing) Growing strong.

triangular (try-ANG-u-lur) Having a shape like a triangle.

tribes (TRYBZ) Groups of people sharing the same customs, language, and ancestors.

Index

Web Sites

To learn more about Jamestown, check out this Web site:
http://www.owlschool.com/williamsburg.html

8/11

9